**CCSS** **Genre** Realistic Fict...

MW00578593

 Essential Question
What can traditions teach you about cultures?

Dragons
on the Water

by Paul Mason
illustrated by Sean O'Neill

Chapter 1
At Chang's House 2

Chapter 2
Dragons and Boats 5

Chapter 3
Ready to Race 9

Chapter 4
And They're Off! 12

Respond to Reading 16

PAIRED READ **A Great Tradition** 17

Focus on Social Studies 20

Chapter 1
At Chang's House

The boys raced up Chang's driveway with their schoolbags dangling from their backs. The wheels of their skateboards made the only sound in the quiet street.

"I led all the way," Joe said, kicking up his board.

"Yeah, right," Chang replied with a laugh. "Mom is still catching up."

The boys dumped their things in the hallway, and Chang went to say hello to his dog, Pepper.

Joe liked coming over to Chang's house because it was very different from his home. It was always entertaining.

Joe walked into the den where Chang's grandfather was sitting on the sofa with a photo album open on his lap.

"Hi, Joe, how are you today?" Chang's grandfather asked.

"I'm fine, Mr. Liu," Joe replied. "What are you looking at?" Joe pointed at a faded color photo of a dragon's head.

"Ah, these are my precious dragon boat pictures from when I was a young man," the old man grinned. "They remind me of when I used to race. Sit down and take a look."

Chang stuck his head around the door. "Come on, Joe. Let's shoot some hoops," he said.

Joe shook his head. "I want to take a look at these first."

"Not those old photos again, Granddad," Chang said, barely hiding his disappointment. "I'll be out in the yard, Joe."

Chapter 2
Dragons and Boats

Chang's grandfather flipped through the photo album.

"Back in Hong Kong, I entered lots of dragon boat races. We won a few, too," he said with pride.

He pointed at one of the photographs. "See all the boats lined up in the water ready to race," he said. "Sometimes there would be thirty boats racing!"

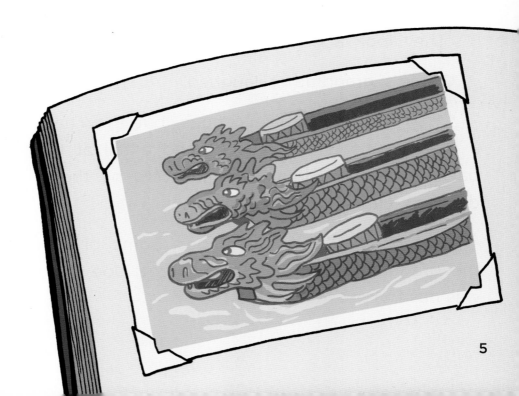

Joe stared intently at the boats and their crews, sitting with their paddles reaching forward. They were poised and ready to go.

"They look a bit like long canoes."

Chang's grandfather laughed.

"They are a little like canoes, but they have a dragon's head at the front and a tail at the back, and the paddles are meant to be the dragon's claws."

He turned a few more pages. Some of the dragons looked extremely fierce. Joe was fascinated.

"Because dragons are a symbol of strength, they're very important in Chinese culture," said Chang's grandfather. "In ancient China, dragon boat races were held to bring farmers good luck and plenty of rain for their crops."

Chang's grandfather suddenly clapped his hands.

"But that's enough of me talking. I've just had an idea. Why don't I take you and Chang to some dragon boat races so you can see them for yourself! There's a dragon boat festival coming up next weekend."

"Really?" Joe said, beaming. "That would be great. I'll go and tell Chang!"

"You might have a struggle to convince him to come, though," Chang's grandfather added with a smile.

Mr. Liu was right. Chang did need to be convinced to go to the dragon boat races.

"I've heard my grandfather's stories about dragon boat racing a million times," he said. "It's so boring. Enough already."

"Aw, come on," said Joe. "All those boats flying up the river will be really exciting."

Chang shrugged his shoulders. "Well, I'll go if you really want, as long as you shoot some hoops with me," he said.

Joe grinned. "Just watch me," he said, grabbing the ball from Chang and shooting a basket.

Chapter 3
Ready to Race

The next weekend, Chang's grandfather took the boys to the Dragon Boat Festival. It was being held in the park by the river. The park was filled with so many people and stalls that it looked like a mini city had sprung up to celebrate the dragon boat races. Tasty smells of food cooking floated on the air, and music played over a massive sound system. People strolled past eating rice cakes wrapped in leaves.

"Those rice cakes are a festival tradition," Chang's grandfather explained.

Down on the boat ramp, there were at least a dozen dragon boats, each one over 40 feet long. Up close, they were bigger and more majestic than either of the boys had thought they would be. The teams were much larger, too—there were over twenty members in each.

Even Chang was intrigued. "I didn't realize there would be so many people here."

His grandfather smiled, "Many people in our community want to take part in this tradition, Chang, because tradition is precious to us."

The crews began warming up, each team huddling in a group, chanting, and getting into the right spirit for the race.

Chang's grandfather looked as if he wished he were down there among them. He patted Chang on the shoulder.

"Being on a dragon boat teaches you how important it is to work together. There's strength through acting as a team."

Joe pointed to a team dressed all in blue. "I know some of those guys," he said. "They come from our neighborhood, and most of them work at the big supermarket."

"Yes," said Chang. "There's Michael Yee—his brother is in our class."

Chapter 4
And They're Off!

Chang's grandfather and the two boys found a good spot to watch the race. Chang felt a tingle of excitement.

"I hope the blue team wins," he said.

"Me, too," replied Joe.

The crowd and crews became quiet—there was an air of expectation as everyone waited for the race to start.

The paddlers faced the front, ready with their paddles raised. The drummers sat at the front of the boats, each with a large drum between his or her legs.

"The drummers are the heartbeat of the boat," Chang's grandfather whispered. "Their rhythm helps keep the paddlers in time, and the drumming is exciting. It builds up your courage. When you hear it, you want to paddle harder!"

The drummers raised their sticks expectantly, ready to strike. Then a loud horn blasted, and they were off—arms pumping hard, paddles a blur of color, and drums thudding. The water around them was churning white as the paddles broke the surface.

Slowly, the pack began to spread out, and three boats surged into the lead. The crowd roared.

"There's the blue team!" shouted Joe.

"They're all close! Come on, blue!" Chang yelled, jumping out of his seat.

Two boats were neck and neck at the front, like racehorses tearing down the homestretch. One was the blue team! The paddlers were giving it all they could.

Ever so slowly, the blue team was inching ahead of the other boat. Chang, Joe, and Chang's grandfather were all cheering. Then, at last, the boats crossed the finish line. The blue team raised their paddles in the air.

"So what did you think of your first dragon boat race?" said Chang's grandfather as the cheering and applause quieted down. "Do you want to come back again next year?"

"For sure," said Joe.

Chang nodded. "Me, too. I was just thinking, Granddad...," said Chang hesitantly, "is there any chance you could get us on one of those boats?"

"Well let's go over and talk to them," said Chang's grandfather with a laugh. "Maybe in a few years' time, you and Joe can join a team and enter the races yourselves!"

Respond to Reading

Summarize

Use details from the story to summarize what happens in *Dragons on the Water*. Your graphic organizer may help you.

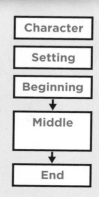

Text Evidence

1. How can you tell if this story is fiction? Which parts are probably true, and which parts are made up? GENRE

2. What happens in the beginning of the story when Joe talks to Chang's grandfather? SEQUENCE

3. What does *fascinated* on page 6 mean? Use the meaning of the other sentences to help you figure it out. SENTENCE CLUES

4. Write about the sequence of events that cause Chang to change his mind about dragon boat racing. WRITE ABOUT READING

Compare Texts
Read about the tradition of dragon boat racing.

A GREAT TRADITION

The tradition of dragon boat racing started almost 2,000 years ago in China. Dragon boat races celebrated the planting of the rice crop in summer.

You can see dragon boats in action in many countries around the world today.

In China, the dragon is an important symbol of strength and power.

So Hing-Keung/Corbis

Dragon boats have brightly colored dragons' heads and tails. The dragon is an important symbol in China. Traditionally, a Chinese dragon is made up of parts of other animals. These can include the head of a camel, the antlers of a deer, the claws of an eagle, and the scales of a fish!

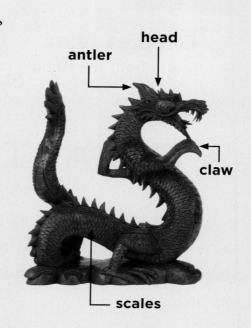

antler

head

claw

scales

Before the race, the dragon boat has to be "woken up," or made ready to race. In a special ceremony, the dragon's eyes are painted with a dot.

Painting the dragon's eye is said to wake the sleeping dragon.

A dragon boat crew works together to race the boat. Each boat usually has 20 paddlers who sit side by side in rows of two. There is also someone at the back to steer the boat, and a drummer at the front who sets the pace.

Dragon boat racing is a fast-growing sport. Going to watch these dragons on the water is a fun way to celebrate this exciting part of Chinese culture.

All over the world, people take part in dragon boat races.

Make Connections

What did reading about the dragon boat tradition tell you about Chinese culture? ESSENTIAL QUESTION

How did the information in *A Great Tradition* help you understand more about the story *Dragons on the Water*? TEXT TO TEXT

Focus on
Social Studies

Purpose To understand the place of traditions in a culture.

Procedure

Step 1 ▶ Research another sport or activity that has come from a specific culture, for example, judo from Japan, lacrosse from Native American tribes, or yoga from India.

Step 2 ▶ Find out what the activity teaches us about the culture it comes from.

Step 3 ▶ Write a description of the activity, giving instructions on how to do it. Use illustrations to support the description. Remember to explain what the activity teaches us about the culture.

Step 4 ▶ Present your description to the class. If possible, arrange for a demonstration. You could also teach others how to play the sport or carry out the activity.